The Life and Work of...

Paul Cézanne

Sean Connolly

Heinemann Library
Des Plaines, Illinois

© 2000 Reed Educational & Professional Publishing
Published by Heinemann Library,
an imprint of Reed Educational & Professional Publishing,
1350 East Touhy Avenue, Suite 240 West
Des Plaines, IL 60018

Customer Service 1-888-454-2279

Designed by Celia Floyd
Illustrations by Karin Littlewood
Printed in Hong Kong, China

04 03 02 01 00
10 9 8 7 6 5 4 3 2 1

Library of Congress Cataloging-in-Publication Data
Connolly, Sean, 1956-
      Paul Cezanne / Sean Connolly.
         p. cm. – (The life and work of--) (Heinemann profiles)
      Includes bibliographical references and index.
      Summary: Introduces the life and work of Paul Cezanne, discussing
his early years, life in Paris, and development as a painter.
      ISBN 1-57572-957-1 (lib. binding)
      1. Cezanne, Paul, 1839-1906 Juvenile literature. 2. Painters
—France Biography Juvenile literature. [1. Cezanne, Paul,
1839-1906. 2. Artists. 3. Painting, french. 4. Art appreciation.]
I. Title. II. Series. III. Series: Heinemann profiles.
ND553.C33C58 1999
759.4—dc21
      [B]   99-14545
                                                                              CIP

Acknowledgments
The Publishers would like to thank the following for permission to reproduce photographs:

Page 4, Portrait photograph of Paul Cézanne, 1889; Credit: AKG. Page 5, Paul Cézanne, *Self-Portrait with Beret*, Credit: B. & U. International Picture Service. Page 7, Paul Cézanne, *Sketchbook Studies*, Credit: R.M.N/Michele Bellot. Page 9, Paul Cézanne, *Paul Alexis Reading to Emile Zola*, Credit: Giraudon. Page 11, Paul Cézanne, *Portrait of Pissarro*, Credit: Giraudon. Page 12, Boulevard des Capucines, Credit: Hulton Getty. Page 13, Paul Cézanne, *Landscape, Auvers*, Credit: Philadelphia Museum of Art. Page 15, Paul Cézanne, *L'Etang des Sœurs, Orsy*, Credit: Courtauld Institute. Page 17, Paul Cézanne, *The Blue Vase*, Credit: Giraudon. Page 19, Paul Cézanne, *The Pool at the Jas de Bouffan*, Credit: Metroplitan Museum of Art. Page 21, Paul Cézanne, *The Card Players*, Credit: The Bridgeman Art Library/Metropolitan Museum of Art. Page 23, Cézanne, *La Montagne Sainte-Victoire*, Credit: National Gallery of Scotland. Page 25, Paul Cézanne, *Portrait of Ambroise Vollard*, Credit: Giraudon. Page 26, Mont Sainte-Victoire, Credit: Corbis. Page 27, Paul Cézanne, *Mont Sainte-Victoire*, Credit: Philadelphia Museum of Art. Page 28, Portrait photograph of Cézanne in front of the picture *Grand Bathers*, Credit: Giraudon. Page 29, Paul Cézanne, *En Bateau*, Credit: National Museum of Western Art, Tokyo.

Cover photograph reproduced with permission of Index/Bridgeman Art Library.

Our thanks to Paul Flux for his comments in the preparation of this book.

Every effort has been made to contact copyright holders of any material reproduced in this book. Any omissions will be rectified in subsequent printings if notice is given to the Publisher.

Some words in this book are in bold, **like this.** You can find out what they mean by looking in the glossary.

Contents

Who Was Paul Cézanne?

Paul Cézanne was a painter. He used colors and shapes to paint pictures of nature. He helped change the way artists see and paint the things around them.

Cézanne painted this **portrait** of himself when he was about 60 years old. By that time, his ideas about painting had already changed the world of art.

Early Years

Paul Cézanne was born January 19, 1839 in Aix-en-Provence, France. One of his childhood friends was named Emile Zola. The boys loved to hike in the countryside near their homes.

Paul **studied** drawing when he was a teenager. He often drew pictures on his walks in the country. These drawings show how he was interested in nature.

Life in Paris

Paul wanted to be an artist. His father wanted him to be a lawyer. When Paul was 22 years old, his father gave him money to move to Paris and become a painter.

8

Paul's friend Emile Zola had become a famous writer in Paris. He liked Paul's work. He told other people about it. This painting shows a friend of Paul's reading to Emile.

Swapping Ideas

In Paris, Paul became friends with a painter named Camille Pissarro. They would go to Camille's country house and paint outside. These trips reminded Paul of home.

Paul did this **sketch** of Camille Pissarro in 1874. It shows how the painters would pack their things and hike to a favorite spot to paint.

Brush with Fame

Painters called the **Impressionists** liked Paul's paintings. They showed two of Paul's paintings at their first **exhibit** in 1874 in Paris. The exhibit was in a building on this street.

This **landscape** was shown at the exhibit. It
shows how Paul used strong colors. The patches
of light and dark show the shapes of the houses.

Ideas of His Own

Paul wanted to try different ways of painting. Patterns of color and shape were more important to him than exact copies of a **scene**.

Paul did this painting when he was 38 years old. He used thick, rough patches of paint to show how he saw this woodland pond.

Between Two Worlds

Paul **studied** the work of the great artists of the past. He liked the French and Dutch **masters** who had lived more than 200 years before him.

The artists of the past loved **still life** painting. Paul's painting of this blue vase shows that he loved still life painting, too.

New Freedom

Paul's father died in 1886. Paul **inherited** enough money to live well. He did not have to worry about whether people would buy his paintings or not.

Paul was free to do the paintings he wanted to do—in new ways! Paul used small blocks of color to make this **landscape** painting.

Ordinary People

Even though Paul was rich, he still thought of himself as ordinary. He painted other ordinary people and used his ideas about color and shape.

This is one of many pictures Paul painted of card players. Although he was painting people, Paul saw the **scene** as a pattern of colors.

Southern Sunshine

Paul began to spend more time near his childhood home. He **studied** the way that the sun changed the color of the countryside.

22

Paul liked to paint this mountain called Mont Sainte-Victoire. This painting shows how he used colors and shapes to show distance.

Turning to People

Ambroise Vollard, an **art dealer** in Paris, had a successful **exhibit** of Paul's paintings in 1895. At the same time, Paul worked on **portraits**.

This is a portrait of Ambroise Vollard. Paul worked hard on each painting. He never finished this one, even though Ambroise had to **pose** for it 115 times!

A Favorite View

Paul worked mainly in southern France. He still painted Mont Sainte-Victoire to show his ideas about color, light, and shape.

This view of the mountain in 1904 shows how Paul's work had changed. The mountain had become just a **blurred** pattern of color.

Cézanne's Last Years

As Paul grew older, he still painted. He even ordered new paintbrushes just before he died. Paul died October 22, 1906. He was 67 years old. By that time, people knew he was a great painter.

In 1905, one year before he died, Paul did this **watercolor** painting. This type of painting was less tiring for Paul as he got older.

Timeline

1839   Paul Cézanne born, January 19

1861   Moves to Paris to become a painter

1861–5 Civil War in the United States

1860s   Learns more about painting from Camille Pissarro

1870–1 War between France and Germany

1871   Begins to paint outside to see light and color more clearly

1874   Has two paintings shown in the first **Impressionist Exhibit**

1876   Alexander Graham Bell invents the telephone

1886   Paul's father dies

1893   First motion picture camera developed in France

1895   Ambroise Vollard sets up one-man exhibit of Cézanne paintings

1902   Builds new **studio** to view Mont Saint-Victoire

1903   Wright brothers fly the first airplane

1906   Paul Cézanne dies, October 22

Glossary

art dealer   someone who sells paintings

blur   to be unclear or fuzzy

exhibit   to show artwork in public

Impressionists   group of artists who painted outside to make colorful pictures

inherit   receive money when someone dies

landscape   painting of the countryside

master   famous artist with great skill

portrait   painting of a person

pose   to sit or stand still for an artist

scene   place where something happens

sketch   rough drawing

still life   painting of things that are set in place by the artist

study   learn about a subject

watercolor   type of paint that is mixed with water and can be used quickly

Index

More Books to Read

Boutan, Mila. *Cézanne.* San Francisco: Chronicle Books, 1996.

Venezia, Mike. *Paul Cézanne.* Danbury, Conn.: Children's Press, 1998.

An older reader can help you with these books.

More Artwork to See

Madame Cézanne in a Striped Skirt, 1877. Museum of Fine Arts, Boston, Mass.

Still Life with Apples and Peaches, 1905. National Gallery of Art, Washington, D.C.

Trees Beside a Stream, 1880–85. Norton-Simon, Los Angeles, Cal.